Library of Congress Catalog Card Number: 71-176358
ISBN: 0-448-02865-4 (Trade Edition)
ISBN: 0-448-03269-4 (Library Edition)
First published by the Hamlyn Publishing Group, Ltd.
© Copyright 1967, Golden Pleasure Books, Ltd.
Published in 1973 in the United States by
Grosset & Dunlap, Inc., New York. All rights reserved.
Printed and bound in the United States.

VERA CROXFORD'S
ANIMALS
EVERYWHERE

Grosset & Dunlap · Publishers · New York

A National General Company

Animals as Pets

PARAKEET / Parakeets come from Australia. They can be tamed and taught to imitate speech. They eat seeds.

WHITE MOUSE / White mice are kept in cages. They hold their food in little pink paws.

GOLDFISH / Goldfish come from China. Sometimes the black and gold ones are just as pretty as the orange and yellow ones. They eat ant eggs and nibble seaweed.

RABBIT / Rabbits have big front teeth for nibbling juicy carrots and lettuce. They are kept in hutches.

TORTOISE / Tortoises nibble leaves and eat worms. They pull their heads and legs inside their shells when they sleep.

CAT / Cats come in all colors and sizes. They are friendly and they love warmth. This is a tortoise-shell cat with pretty markings.

DOG / There are hundreds of different breeds of dogs. Some, like hounds, are hunting dogs. Others are just pets.

Animals on the Farm

PIG / Pigs are kept in sties by farmers. Their tails are curly and they grunt through their noses.

SHEEP / Sheep have thick wool coats which are sheared in the spring. They eat grass.

GOAT / Goats give rich, creamy milk. They butt with their bony heads. They are good at climbing rocks.

BULL / The fierce bull is always kept fenced in. Although it only eats grass, it is very strong.

DUCK / Ducks have oily feathers so that water runs right off them. On land they enjoy waddling in the mud.

HORSE / Horses are strong and can pull heavy loads. Horses that work on farms are called draft horses. They love to munch juicy carrots.

HEN / Hens stay in the barnyard and lay eggs for us to eat.

ROOSTERS / Roosters crow at daybreak. They are the farmer's "alarm clock."

COW / A cow eats grass and gives us milk to drink. It is gentle and soft-eyed.

GOOSE / A goose hisses when it is angry. It can honk like an automobile horn, too.

Pond and Woodland Animals

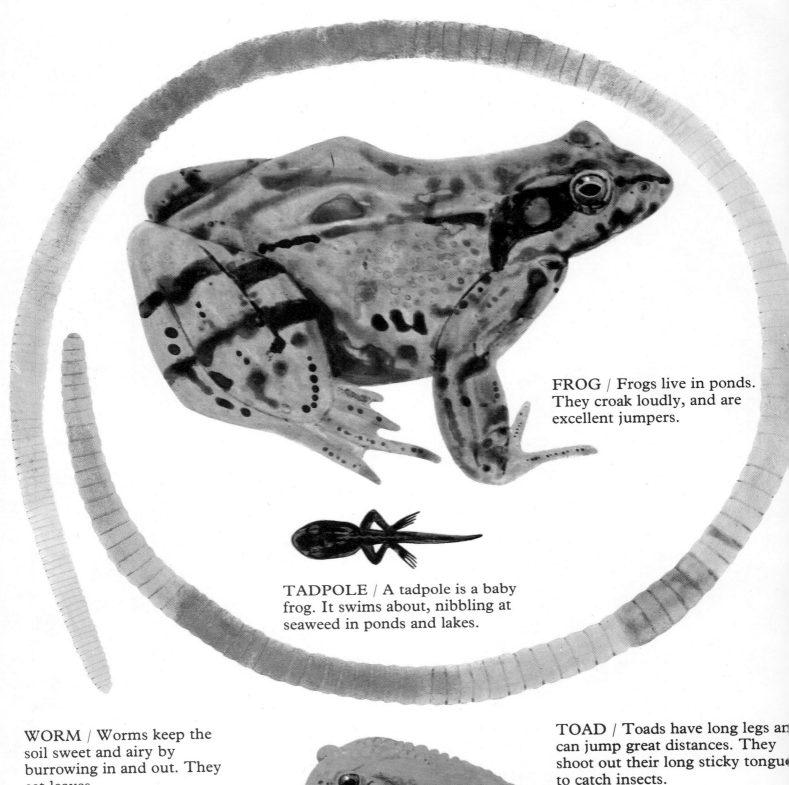

FROG / Frogs live in ponds. They croak loudly, and are excellent jumpers.

TADPOLE / A tadpole is a baby frog. It swims about, nibbling at seaweed in ponds and lakes.

WORM / Worms keep the soil sweet and airy by burrowing in and out. They eat leaves.

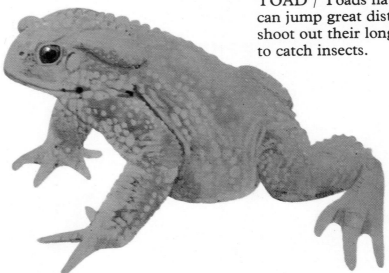

TOAD / Toads have long legs and can jump great distances. They shoot out their long sticky tongue to catch insects.

STARLING / Starlings eat many of our garden pests. They fly about in flocks, chattering noisily.

SPARROW / Sparrows are bold little birds. They eat worms, as well as bread and cake crumbs.

SLUG / Slugs are slimy and are found in the shade. They eat young, juicy vegetable leaves.

SNAIL / Snails move slowly. They carry their shell-houses on their back. Their eyes are at the end of their horns.

Birds and Insects

BUMBLEBEE / Bumblebees are very large bees. They do not live in hives. They build nests.

HONEYBEE / Honeybees live in hives. They make honey with nectar gathered from flowers. They sting when they are frightened.

WASP / Wasps build nests in tree trunks. In the autumn, they eat ripe fruit.

TAWNY OWL / The Tawny Owl lives in trees. It sleeps by day and comes out at night to hunt and catch mice.

LADYBUG / A ladybug is a beetle which flies from plant to plant. It eats tiny insects.

WAXWING / Waxwings fly together in big flocks. They eat berries and other fruits.

EARWIG / Earwigs are insects that live in the bark of trees. Sometimes they sun themselves on the leaves of plants. They eat flies.

THRUSH / Thrushes have a clear, sweet song. They like to eat worms and snails.

Garden Animals

SPIDER / Spiders spin webs to catch their food, usually flies. They wait in the center of the web for insects to be caught in the strands.

ANT / Ants are small, busy insects. They build nests in the earth called ant hills, which have many rooms.

TREE CREEPER / A tree creeper has sharp claws to grip tree trunks. Its beak is specially curved to peck insects out of bark.

PAINTED LADY / The Painted Lady is a butterfly which lays its eggs on nettles and thistles. It can be seen in the summer, flying over fields, paths and gardens.

GYPSY MOTH / Gypsy moths fly about at night. They lay their eggs on twigs and tree trunks.

CATERPILLAR / Caterpillars eat the leaves of plants. They eventually become butterflies or moths.

Animals of the Field and Hedgerow

SHREW / Shrews are tiny, mouse-like creatures with long noses. They live in hedges and woods, and are not nearly as big as shown here.

VOLE / Voles are like large mice, and they eat grass. They also build their nests out of gra

FIELD MOUSE / A field mouse has a long tail and whiskers. It likes nuts and seeds.

HEDGEHOG / Hedgehogs live under bushes. They curl up and sleep all winter long.

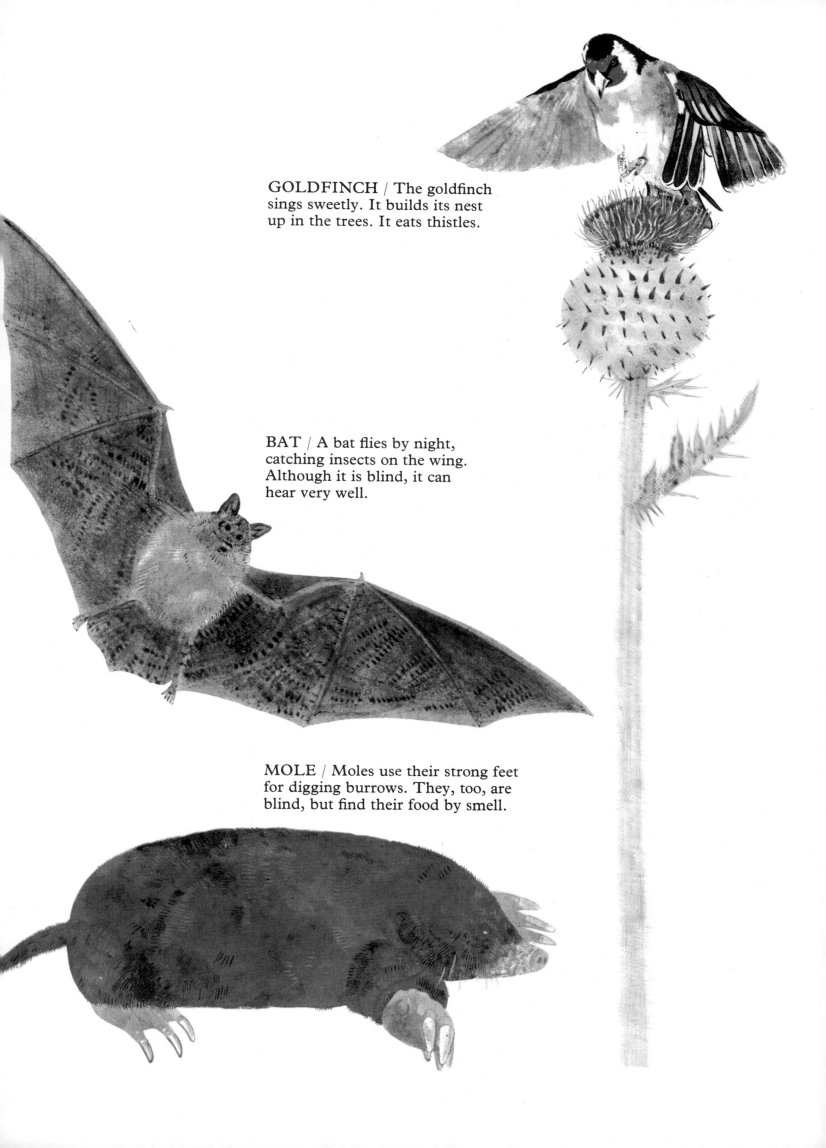

GOLDFINCH / The goldfinch sings sweetly. It builds its nest up in the trees. It eats thistles.

BAT / A bat flies by night, catching insects on the wing. Although it is blind, it can hear very well.

MOLE / Moles use their strong feet for digging burrows. They, too, are blind, but find their food by smell.

European Animals

RED MULLET / Red Mullet live in warm seas and eat tiny plants. Their teeth are very small.

HARVEST MOUSE / A harvest mouse makes its nest among cornstalks. It lives on insects and grain.

OTTER / Otters live in dens river banks. They love to play and splash in the water.

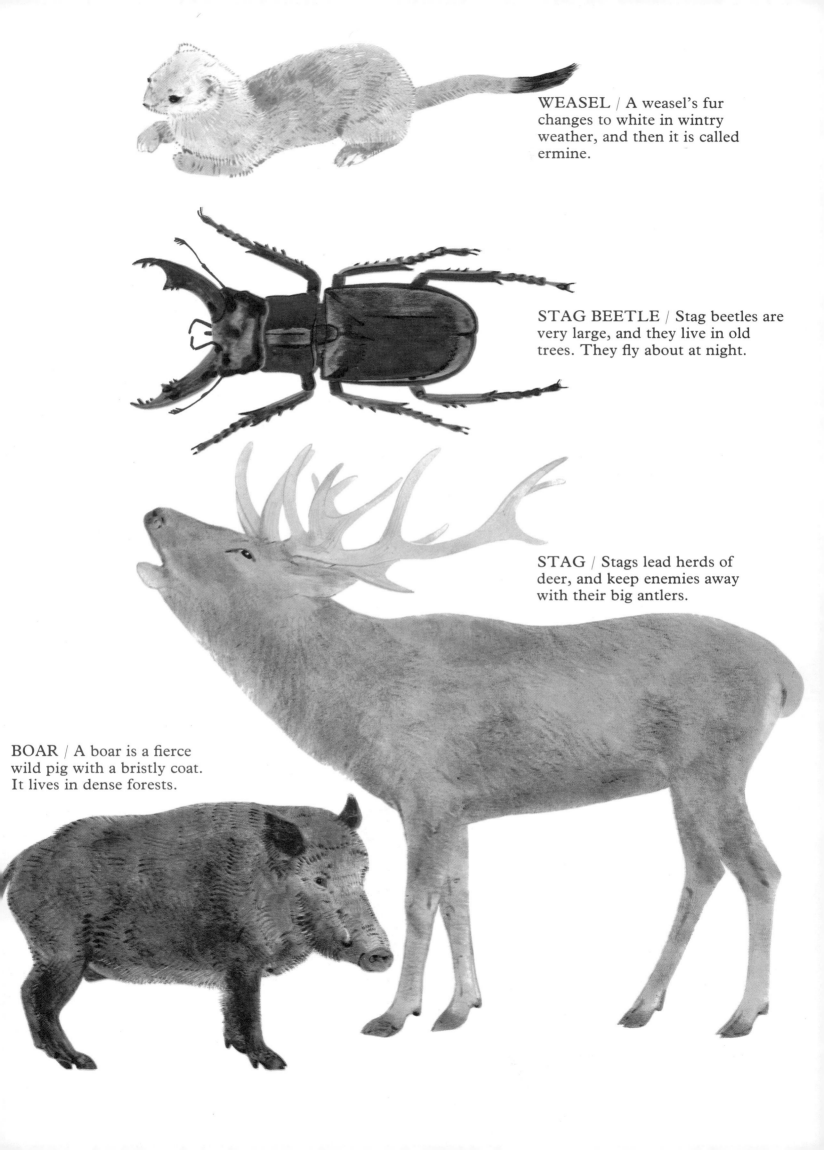

WEASEL / A weasel's fur changes to white in wintry weather, and then it is called ermine.

STAG BEETLE / Stag beetles are very large, and they live in old trees. They fly about at night.

STAG / Stags lead herds of deer, and keep enemies away with their big antlers.

BOAR / A boar is a fierce wild pig with a bristly coat. It lives in dense forests.

European and North American Animals

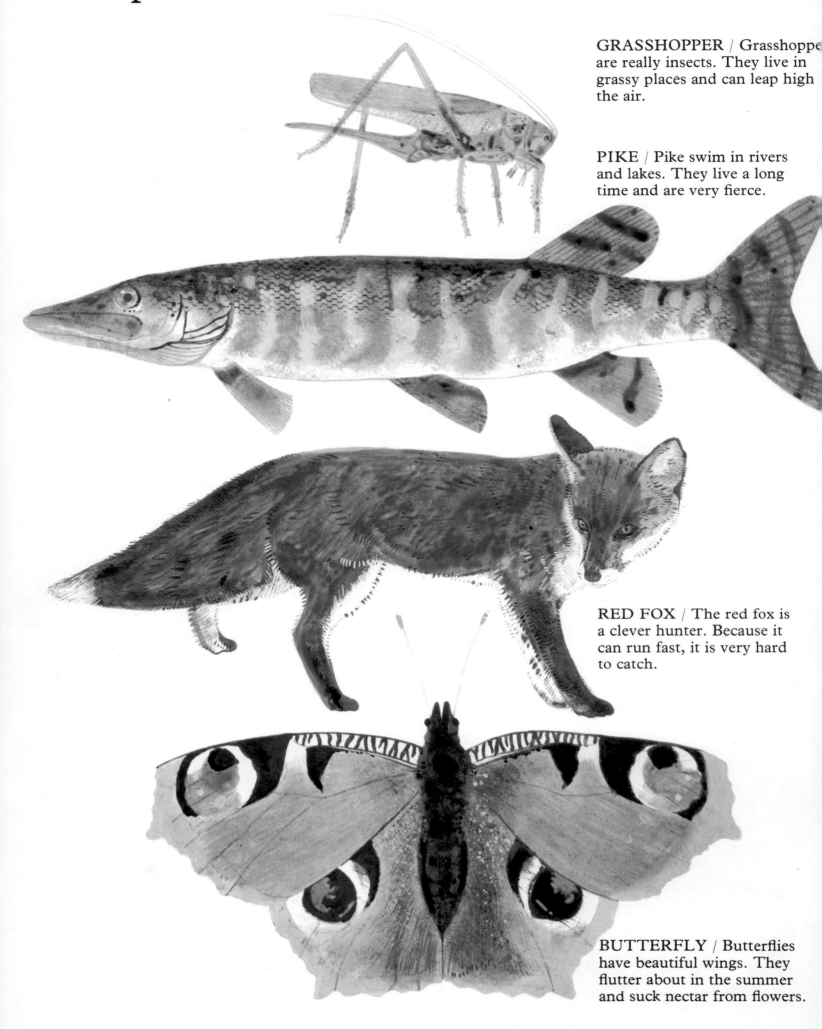

GRASSHOPPER / Grasshoppe[r] are really insects. They live in grassy places and can leap high [in] the air.

PIKE / Pike swim in rivers and lakes. They live a long time and are very fierce.

RED FOX / The red fox is a clever hunter. Because it can run fast, it is very hard to catch.

BUTTERFLY / Butterflies have beautiful wings. They flutter about in the summer and suck nectar from flowers.

DRAGONFLY / Dragonflies have two sets of beautiful shiny wings. They hover over rivers and ponds.

WILD RABBIT / Wild rabbits live in burrows. Their fluffy white tails are used to signal danger. They can run very fast.

KINGFISHER / Kingfishers hover over water and dive to spear fish with their sharp beaks.

European Animals

BULLFINCH / The bullfinch
has a sweet piping call.
It eats insects and seeds.

EUROPEAN BADGER /
European badgers are extremely
clean animals. Their underground
homes are tidied every day.

DORMOUSE / A dormouse makes
a nest in the autumn and sleeps
all winter curled up in a ball.

GRASS SNAKE / Grass snakes
are harmless and are very shy.
They eat small fish and frogs.

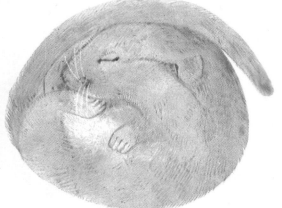

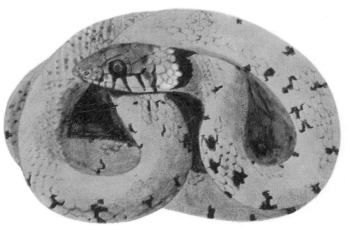

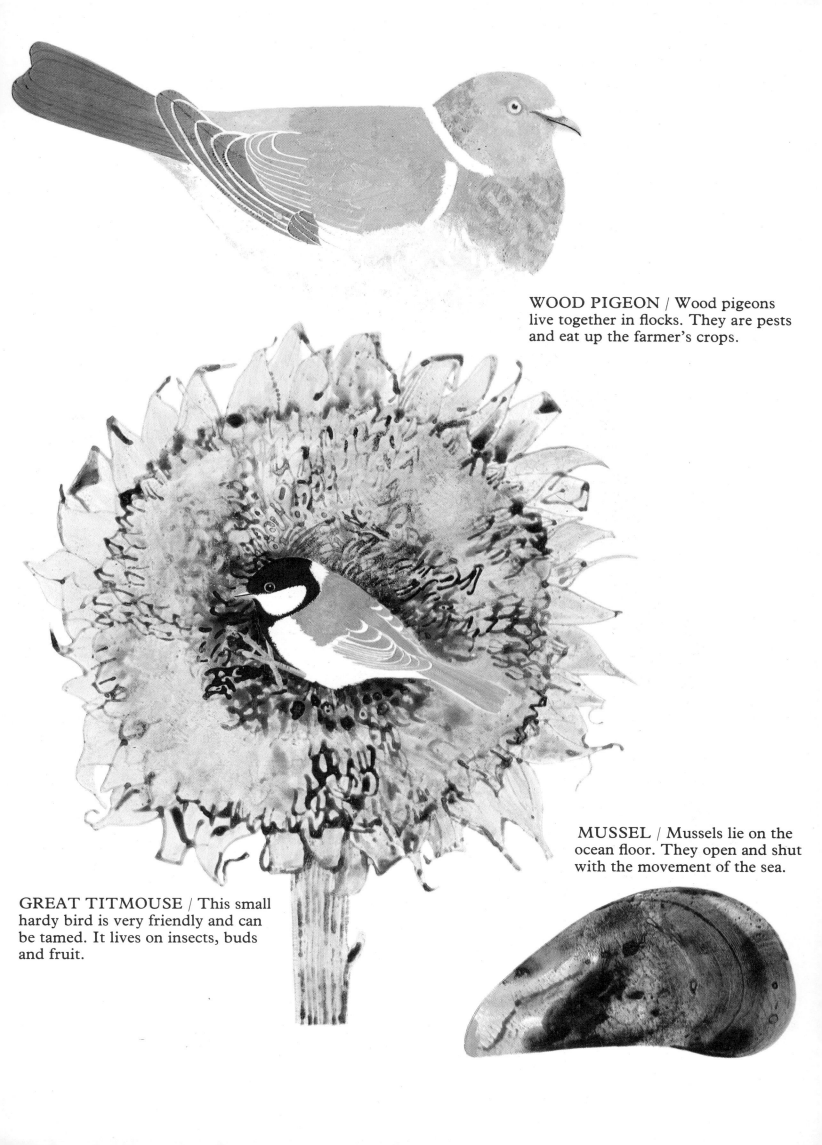

WOOD PIGEON / Wood pigeons live together in flocks. They are pests and eat up the farmer's crops.

MUSSEL / Mussels lie on the ocean floor. They open and shut with the movement of the sea.

GREAT TITMOUSE / This small hardy bird is very friendly and can be tamed. It lives on insects, buds and fruit.

North American Animals

ARMADILLO / The armadillo
is covered with scales. It
burrows long tunnels in the
ground.

SALMON / Salmon are large fish.
They are so strong that
they can leap up waterfalls.

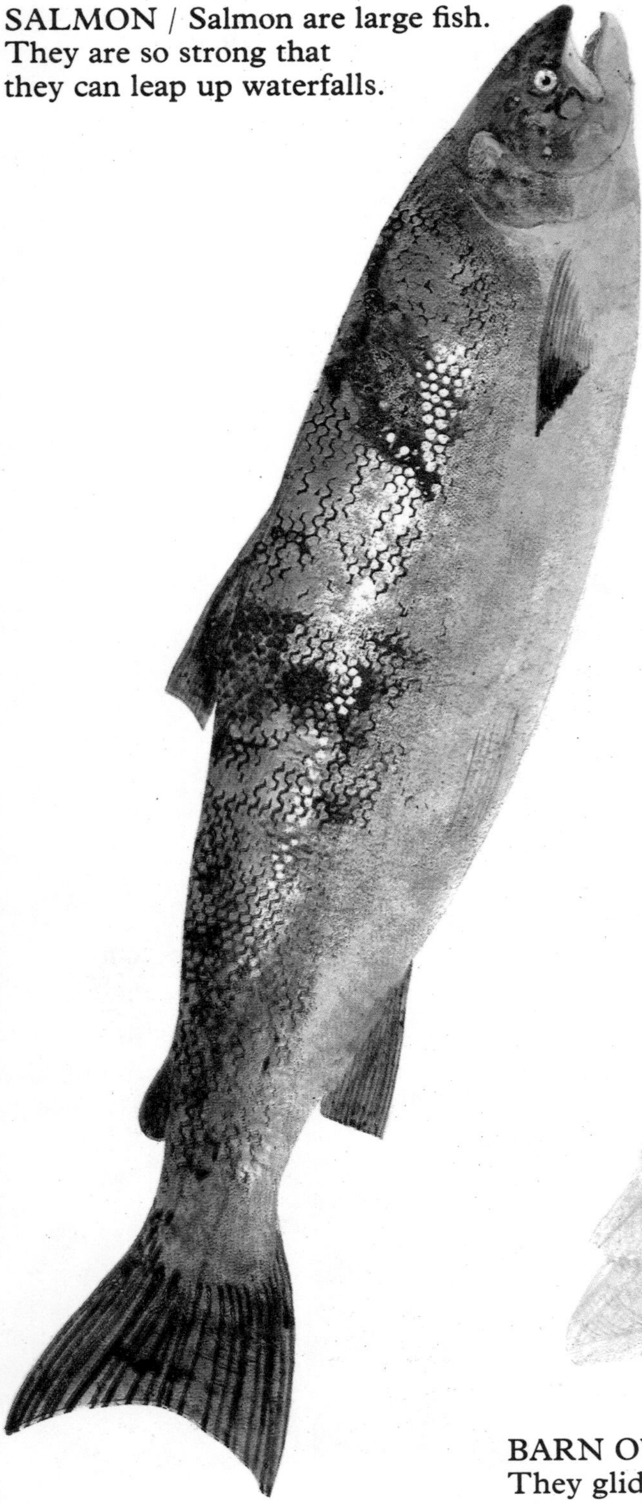

BARN OWL / Barn owls hunt at night.
They glide soundlessly on their wide
wings, catching mice.

RACCOON / The raccoon lives near rivers and lakes. It always washes its food in water before eating it.

WOLVERINE / Wolverines are rare today, but can be found in thick northern forests. They are bold and fearless.

BEAVER / Beavers build dams by setting logs across streams. They play in the water and catch fish.

CROW / Crows eat frogs and insects. They have harsh voices and cry, "Caw-caw" in loud tones.

North American Animals

SQUIRREL / Squirrels live in trees and collect nuts which they bury in the ground and dig up again during the winter.

EEL / The eel is a long, thin fish. It wriggles through the mud at the bottom of rivers.

GRIZZLY BEAR / Grizzly bears are big and fierce. They love honey.

SKUNK / Skunks live near rivers and ponds. When attacked or frightened, they squirt a musky fluid having a disagreeable odor, which often sends their enemies scurrying away.

DOLPHIN / Dolphins are small whales. They love to play games and do funny tricks in the water.

MAGPIE / Magpies chatter in harsh voices. They collect glittering objects to hide in their nests.

EAGLE / Eagles have nests called aeries that are situated high on clifftops. When they are hovering very high, they can see even a tiny mouse on the ground.

North American Animals

MOOSE / The moose is
a type of American deer
with big antlers. Its hide
is thick and tough.

CANADA GOOSE / Canada
geese make their nests in reeds on
the edge of frozen lakes.

HARE / A hare has large hind feet,
which it uses to hop and leap high in
the air.

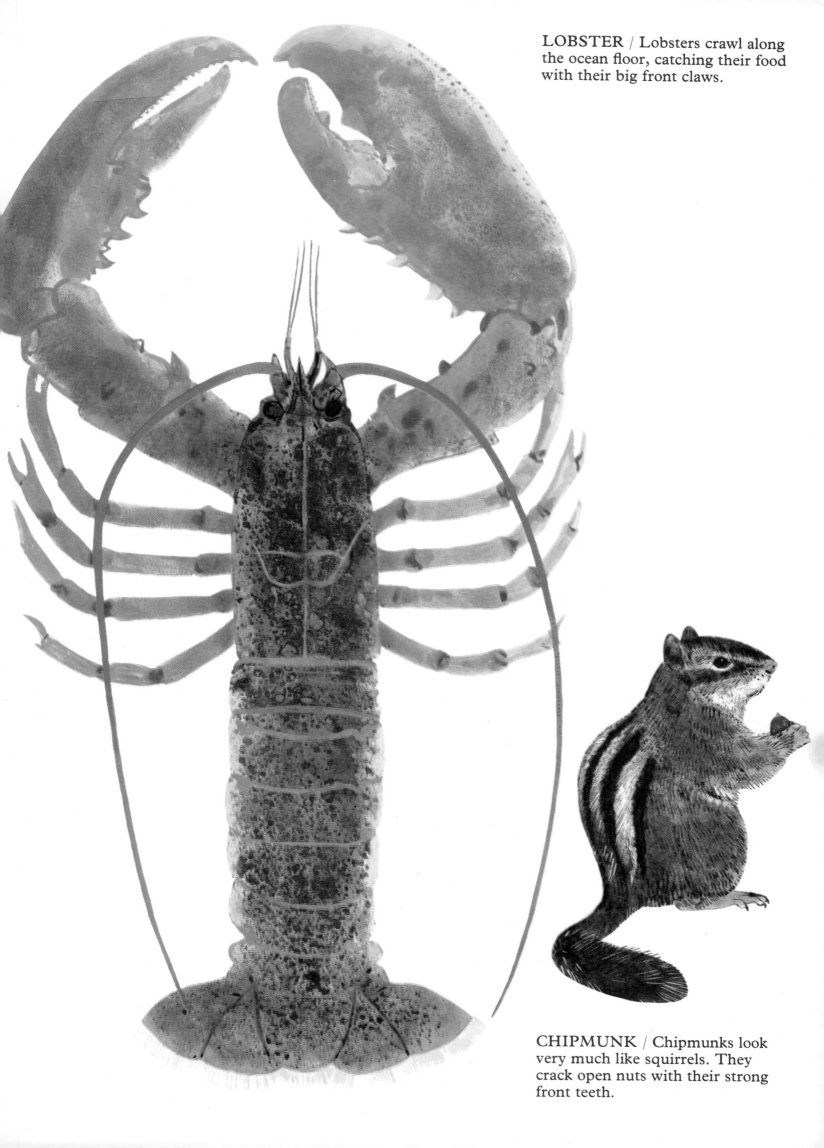

LOBSTER / Lobsters crawl along the ocean floor, catching their food with their big front claws.

CHIPMUNK / Chipmunks look very much like squirrels. They crack open nuts with their strong front teeth.

Animals from Australia

DUCKBILLED PLATYPUS / The platypus lives in streams and ponds. It is very rare and, surprisingly, it lays eggs.

CUSCUS / A cuscus climbs trees by curling its tail around the branches. It eats leaves.

COCKATEEL / Cockateels live in flocks and nest in hollows. They can be tamed and taught to talk.

SPINY ANTEATER / Spiny anteaters spend the day underground, and feed at night on ants and termites.

SUGAR GLIDER / Sugar gliders glide from treetop to ground during the night. They feed on insects.

GOULDIAN FINCH / Gouldian finches live in flocks in open, grassy country. They nest near rivers.

KOALA BEAR / Koalas climb eucalyptus trees and eat the leaves. Baby koalas are carried on their mothers' backs.

Animals from Australia and New Zealand

KANGAROO / Mother kangaroos have pouches in which to carry their babies. They feed on grass and leaves.

WALLABY / Wallabies jump through the air with bounding leaps. They eat fruit and seeds.

TASMANIAN WOLF / The Tasmanian wolf lives on the edge of the forests, and it eats birds, frogs and lizards. It howls at night.

WOMBAT / Wombats sleep during the day in nests lined with bark. They carry their babies in their pouches.

BLACK SWAN / The black swan builds a shallow nest of twigs by the side of a river. Its babies are called cygnets.

EMU / Emus are birds with long legs. They live in flocks. They can't fly, but they can run very fast.

KIWI / Kiwis are very shy birds which live in thick, swampy forests. They have a shrill piping call.

Animals of the African Plains

GIRAFFE / Giraffes are the tallest animals on earth. They eat leaves from the tops of trees.

OSTRICH / Ostriches are bird which cannot fly. They bury the heads in the sand when they are frightened.

GNU / Gnus live close to water holes in African grass country. They travel in large herds.

AFRICAN ELEPHANT
The African elephant has large ears. It has ivory tusks and very tough skin.

GAZELLE / A gazelle is a graceful animal. It leaps high into the air as it runs.

ZEBRA / Most zebras graze on grassy plains. Their striped coats help to hide them from their enemies.

Animals of the African Plains

BUFFALO / A buffalo has curved horns. It likes to stand up to its neck in cool, muddy water.

WART HOG / A wart hog is a wild pig. It lives near water and digs holes in the ground.

CAPE HUNTING DOG / Cape hunting dogs can run very fast. They hunt in packs and live in burrows.

LION / A group of lions living together is called a pride.

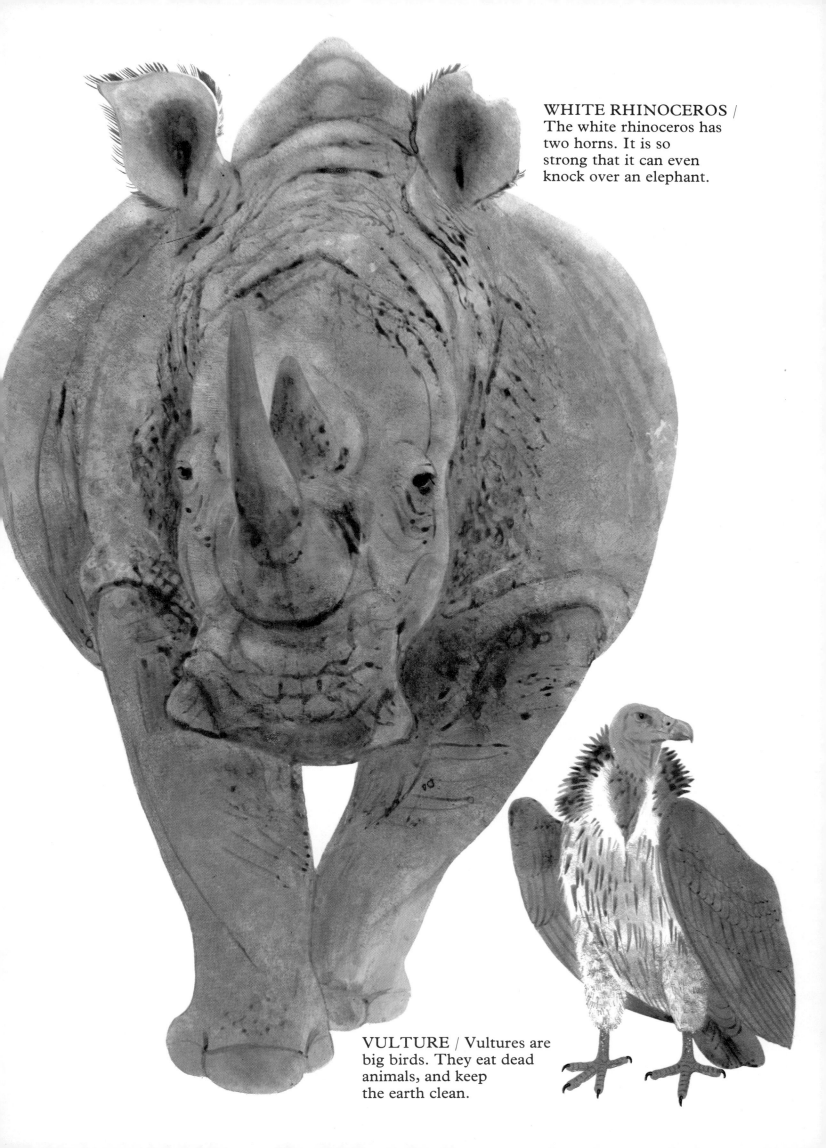

WHITE RHINOCEROS /
The white rhinoceros has
two horns. It is so
strong that it can even
knock over an elephant.

VULTURE / Vultures are
big birds. They eat dead
animals, and keep
the earth clean.

Animals of the American Prairie

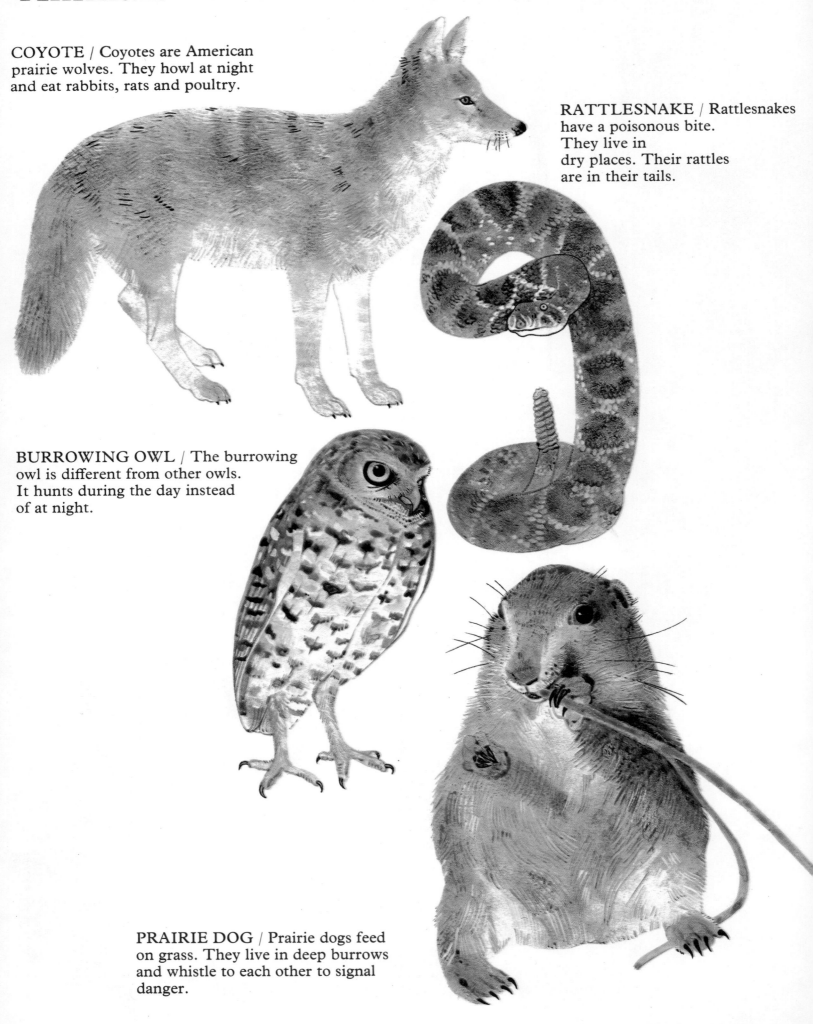

COYOTE / Coyotes are American prairie wolves. They howl at night and eat rabbits, rats and poultry.

RATTLESNAKE / Rattlesnakes have a poisonous bite. They live in dry places. Their rattles are in their tails.

BURROWING OWL / The burrowing owl is different from other owls. It hunts during the day instead of at night.

PRAIRIE DOG / Prairie dogs feed on grass. They live in deep burrows and whistle to each other to signal danger.

CARACARA / Caracaras keep the earth clean by eating up any dead animals they find.

BISON / Bison live in herds on the prairies and have shaggy coats. They eat grass.

AMERICAN BADGER / The badger sleeps during the day and ventures out at night. It eats berries, slugs and snails.

Animals of the Indian Plains

MONGOOSE / The mongoose, though small, is fearless. It fights and kills fierce snakes.

BLACK BUCK / Black buck are antelopes with twisted horns. They jump very high and leap great distances.

CHEETAH / A cheetah is a hunting leopard. It is the fastest animal in the world.

INDIAN RHINOCEROS / The Indian rhinoceros has a single horn made of matted hair. It is used as a weapon of defense.

COBRA / A cobra is one of the deadliest snakes in the world. Its poison kills instantly.

PEACOCK / Peacocks come from India and Ceylon. They have large, beautiful tails and harsh voices.

Animals of Hot Deserts and Dry Places

CAMEL / The camel stores fat in
its hump. It has padded feet for
walking over hot sand. A camel
with one hump is called a
dromedary.

MARABOU STORK / The
marabou stork makes its
nest in the trees and can
fly long distances. It has
soft, downy feathers.

LOCUST / Locusts are pests.
A swarm of them can settle
on a field and gobble up
every leaf and blade of grass.

GERBIL / Gerbils live in sandy places. They jump around with their long legs.

FROG / This frog lives in the desert, and stores water in its body to use during the dry season.

SAIGA / The saiga looks like an antelope, but is really a goat. Its swollen nose keeps sand out.

FENNEC FOX / A fennec fox is a small desert animal. It is very fond of dates and fruit.

Animals of the Cold Mountains

ANDEAN CONDOR / The Andean condor is the largest flying bird in the world. It nests in cliffs.

MOUNTAIN GOAT / The mountain goat leaps from rock to rock with the greatest of ease. It feeds on moss and grass.

LLAMA / Llamas have soft, fine fur. They live high up in the mountains of South America.

BLACK BEAR / Black bears are clever. They catch fish in the river with their paws.

YAK / Yaks live in the mountains of Tibet. They have heavy coats to keep them warm.

PANDA / Pandas are very shy. They live in China and eat bamboo shoots.

African Jungle Animals

GORILLA / A gorilla is
a large ape. It is very strong,
but has a gentle nature.

GRAY PARROT / The gray
parrot lives in hot, wet
forests. It is a clever mimic
and can imitate almost any
sound.

MANDRILL / Mandrills stay
in very thick forests, sleeping
in the trees at night. They
like to eat fruit.

OKAPI / Okapis pick leaves
from trees and bushes
with their long tongues.
They are relatives of
deer and zebras.

CHIMPANZEE / Chimpanzees are
apes. They can learn to do many
clever tricks and are good
imitators of people.

African Jungle Animals

AFRICAN GOLDEN CAT / African golden cats have very long tails. They run fast and are good at climbing trees.

POTTO / The potto, a shy animal, lives in thick forests. It likes to eat insects, lizards and fruit.

PORCUPINE / Porcupines are covered with quills and spines. At night they search for leaves, shoots and bark to eat.

CHAMELEON / A chamele is a tree-climbing lizard. It can change its color to match its background.

HIPPOPOTAMUS / The hippopotamus spends most of its time in cool, muddy waters to escape the hot sun. Although its teeth are large, the hippopotamus eats only grass, weeds and leaves.

Indian Jungle Animals

SLOTH BEAR / The sloth bear is a good climber. It eats fruit, leaves and insects.

LEAF INSECTS / Leaf insects are so much like leaves that even birds can't tell the difference.

FLAMED MINIVET / Flamed minivets live in the jungle, in noisy bands of twenty or more birds.

INDIAN ELEPHANT / The Indian elephant has small ears. It can uproot trees with its strong trunk.

HORNBILL / Hornbills live in thick forests and travel in small flocks. They have very loud voices.

HANUMAN MONKEY / Hanuman monkeys live in packs in the treetops and swing from branch to branch.

TIGER / Tigers are fierce animals. Their stripes make them hard to see in the long grass.

South American Jungle Animals

TAPIR / Tapirs are gentle, piglike creatures. They nibble twigs and fruit with their long snouts.

COCK-OF-THE-ROCK / This bird makes its nest of mud and sticks, decorated with leaves, near jungle streams.

JAGUAR / A jaguar is a fierce wild cat with sharp claws. It is a good swimmer.

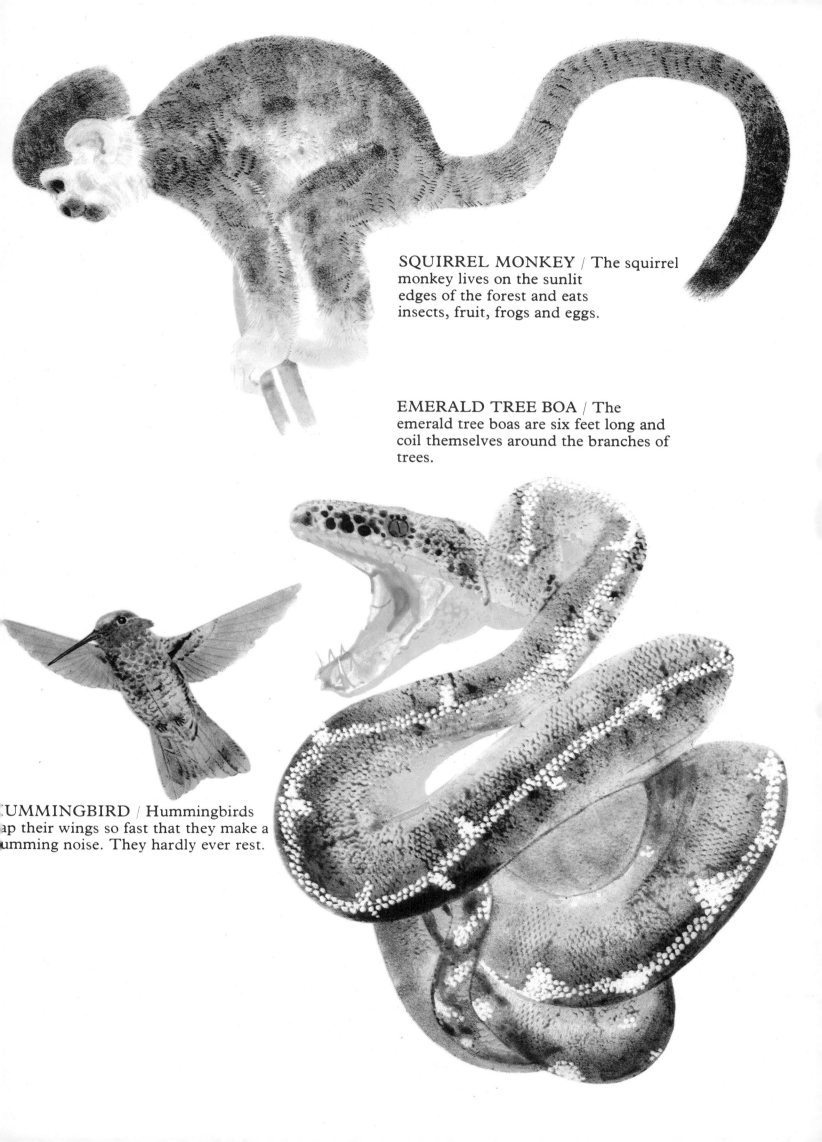

SQUIRREL MONKEY / The squirrel monkey lives on the sunlit edges of the forest and eats insects, fruit, frogs and eggs.

EMERALD TREE BOA / The emerald tree boas are six feet long and coil themselves around the branches of trees.

HUMMINGBIRD / Hummingbirds flap their wings so fast that they make a humming noise. They hardly ever rest.

South American Jungle Animals

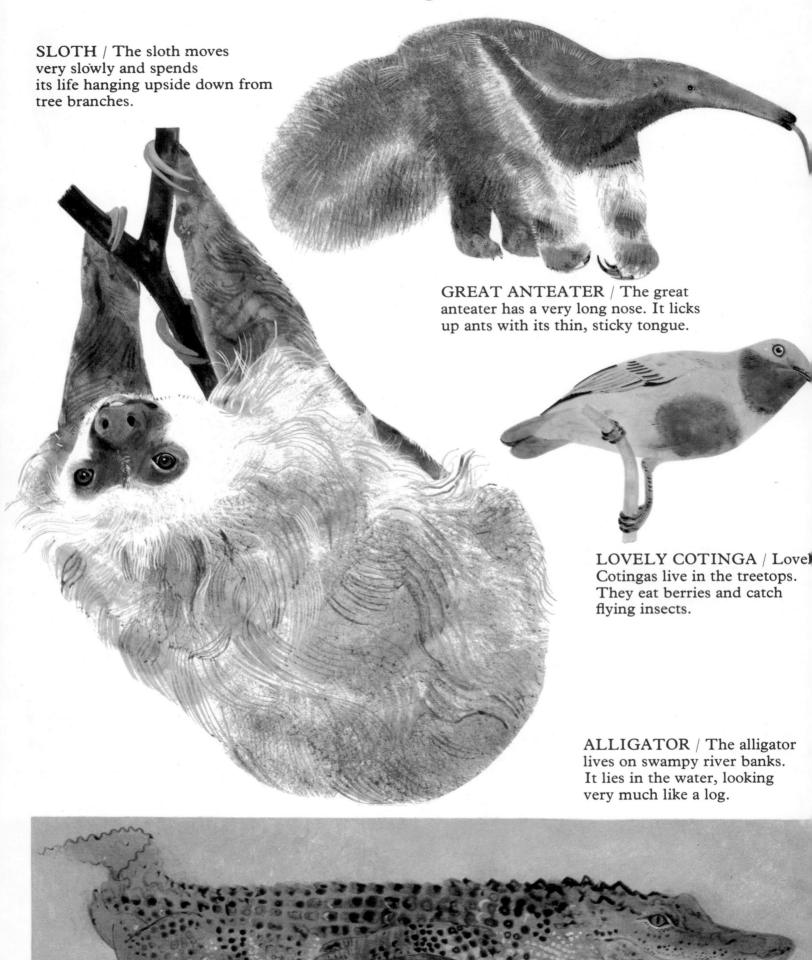

SLOTH / The sloth moves very slowly and spends its life hanging upside down from tree branches.

GREAT ANTEATER / The great anteater has a very long nose. It licks up ants with its thin, sticky tongue.

LOVELY COTINGA / Lovely Cotingas live in the treetops. They eat berries and catch flying insects.

ALLIGATOR / The alligator lives on swampy river banks. It lies in the water, looking very much like a log.

TOUCAN / Toucans are found in the hot, humid jungles of tropical America. They eat fruit and insects. They cannot fly far.

PECCARY / The peccary is a wild pig. Its hide is very thick and tough.

Animals of the Tropical Waters

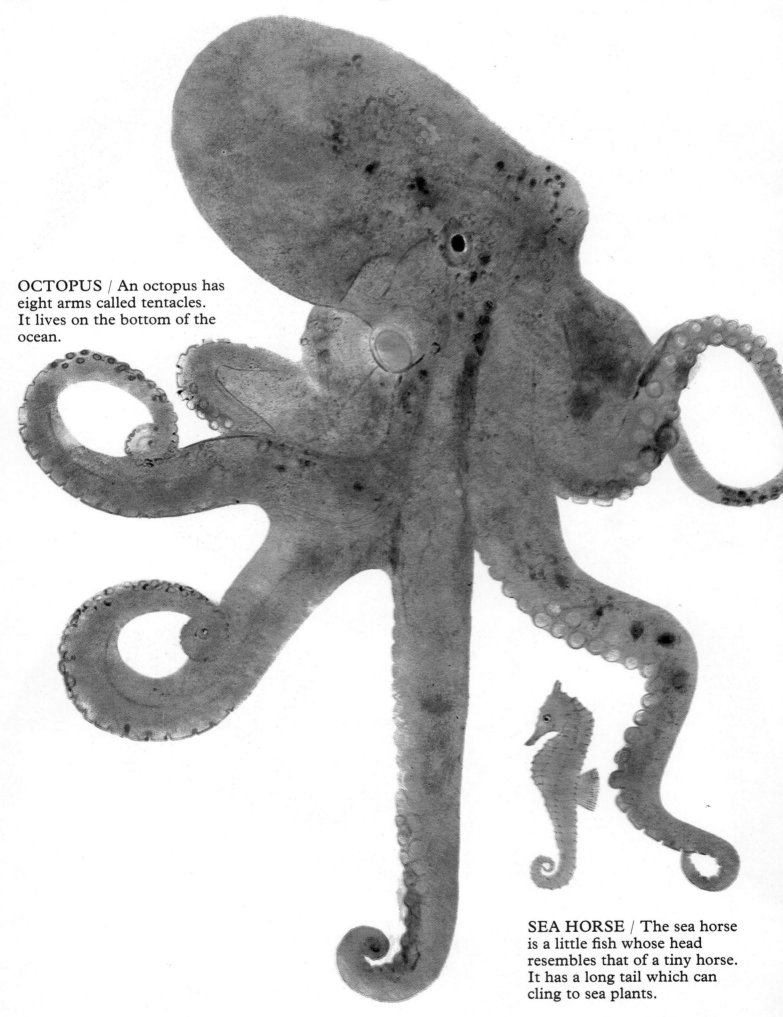

OCTOPUS / An octopus has eight arms called tentacles. It lives on the bottom of the ocean.

SEA HORSE / The sea horse is a little fish whose head resembles that of a tiny horse. It has a long tail which can cling to sea plants.

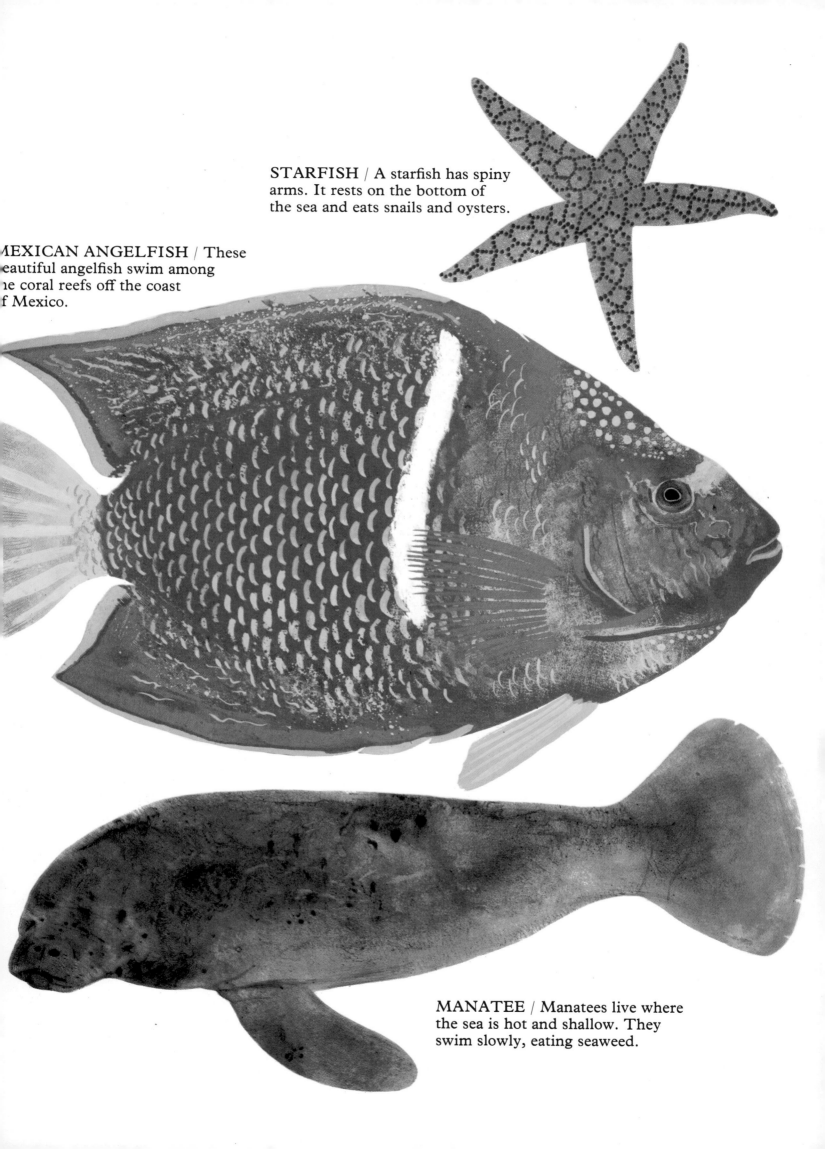

STARFISH / A starfish has spiny arms. It rests on the bottom of the sea and eats snails and oysters.

MEXICAN ANGELFISH / These beautiful angelfish swim among the coral reefs off the coast of Mexico.

MANATEE / Manatees live where the sea is hot and shallow. They swim slowly, eating seaweed.

Animals of the Tropical Waters

SHARK / Sharks are big fish with very sharp teeth. They attack smaller fish and are often a threat to human swimmers and divers.

TURTLE / Turtles swim in warm seas. They often live to be a hundred years old.

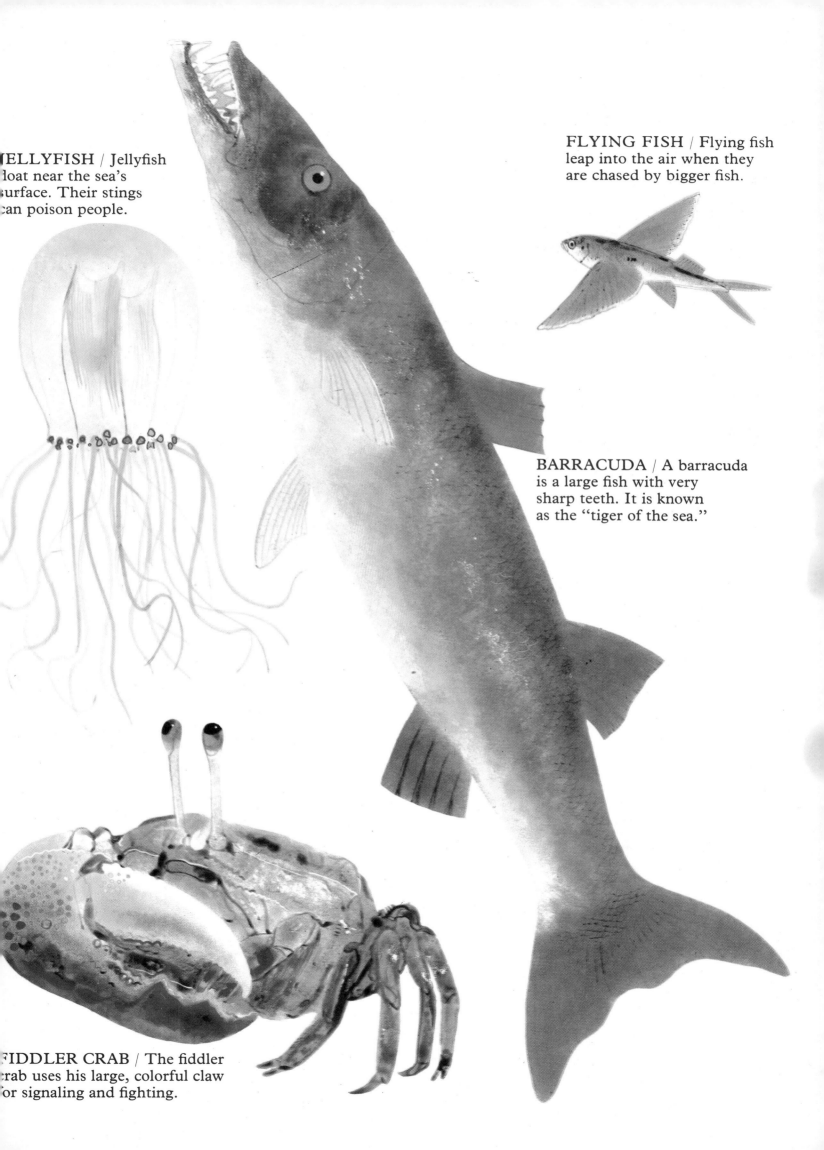

JELLYFISH / Jellyfish float near the sea's surface. Their stings can poison people.

FLYING FISH / Flying fish leap into the air when they are chased by bigger fish.

BARRACUDA / A barracuda is a large fish with very sharp teeth. It is known as the "tiger of the sea."

FIDDLER CRAB / The fiddler crab uses his large, colorful claw for signaling and fighting.

Animals of the Frozen North

WALRUS / Walruses make loud bellowing noises. They feed on clams which they find on the bottom of the ocean.

SEAL / Seals are peaceful animals. They bask on the beach and frolic in the water.

WHALE / Whales swim together in "schools." They are very strong and, unlike fish, have warm blood.

ARCTIC FOX / The arctic fox burrows in the snow to make a den for rearing its young.

SNOWY OWL / Snowy owls' feathers are tipped with white so that they do not show against the snow.

MUSK OX / The musk ox lives in very cold countries. Its thick coat of hair keeps it warm.

POLAR BEAR / Polar bears live near the North Pole amid ice and snow. They are very good swimmers.

REINDEER / Reindeer are found in the far icy North. They search for moss to eat by clearing away the snow with their front hoofs.